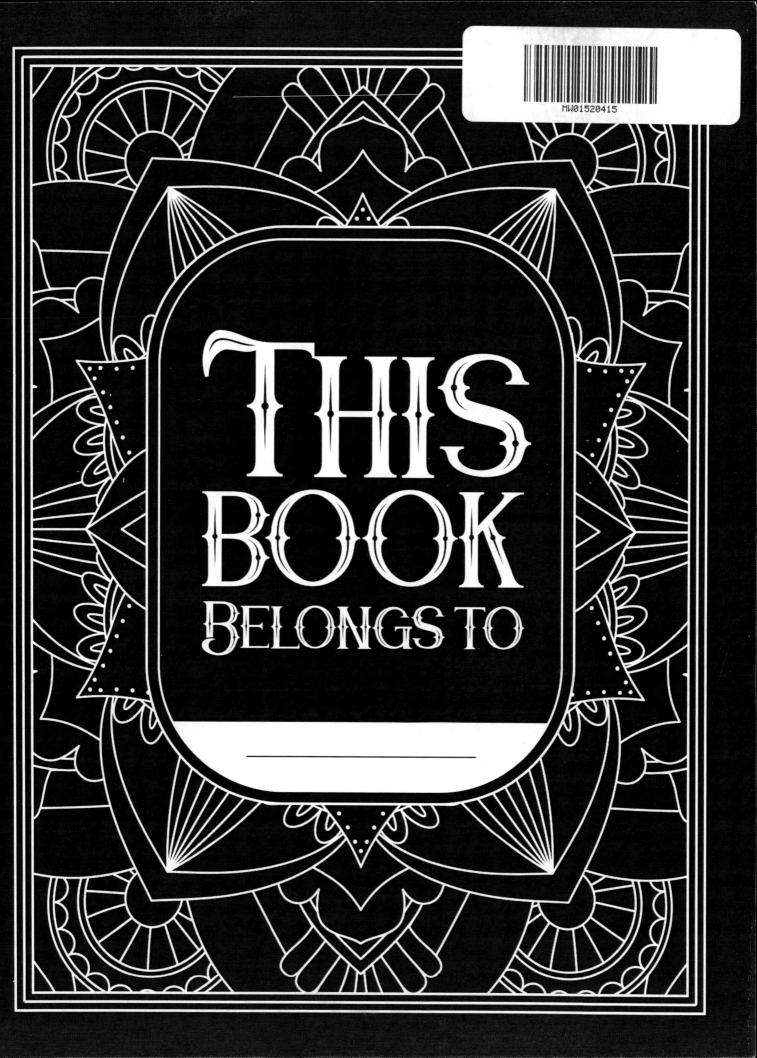

THIS
BOOK
BELONGS TO

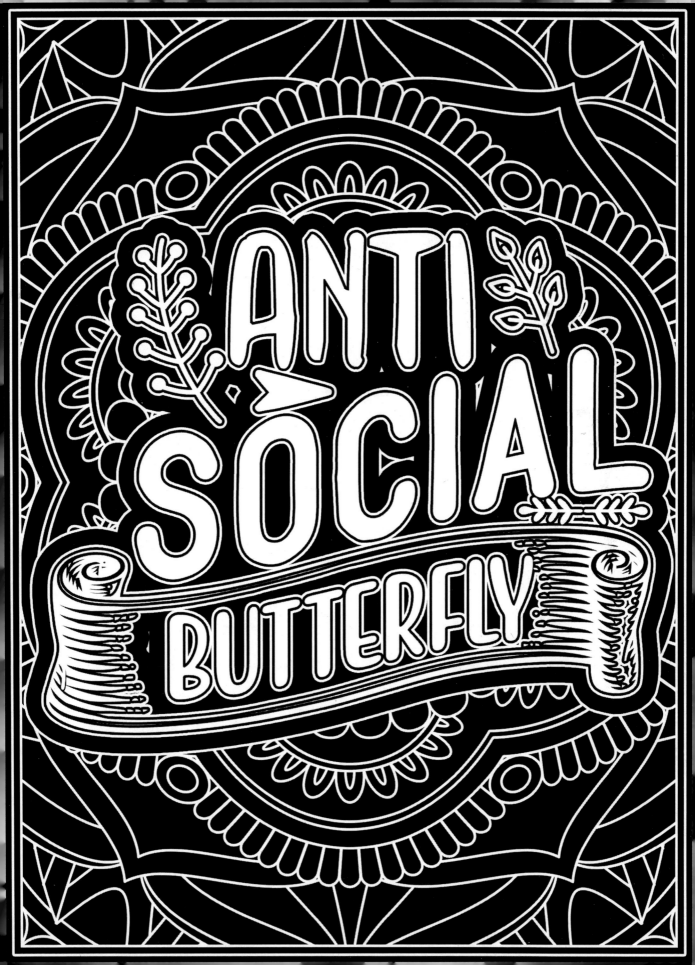

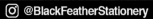

Tag us on your finished pages
for a free shoutout

@BlackFeatherStationery

Tag us on your finished pages
for a free shoutout

@BlackFeatherStationery

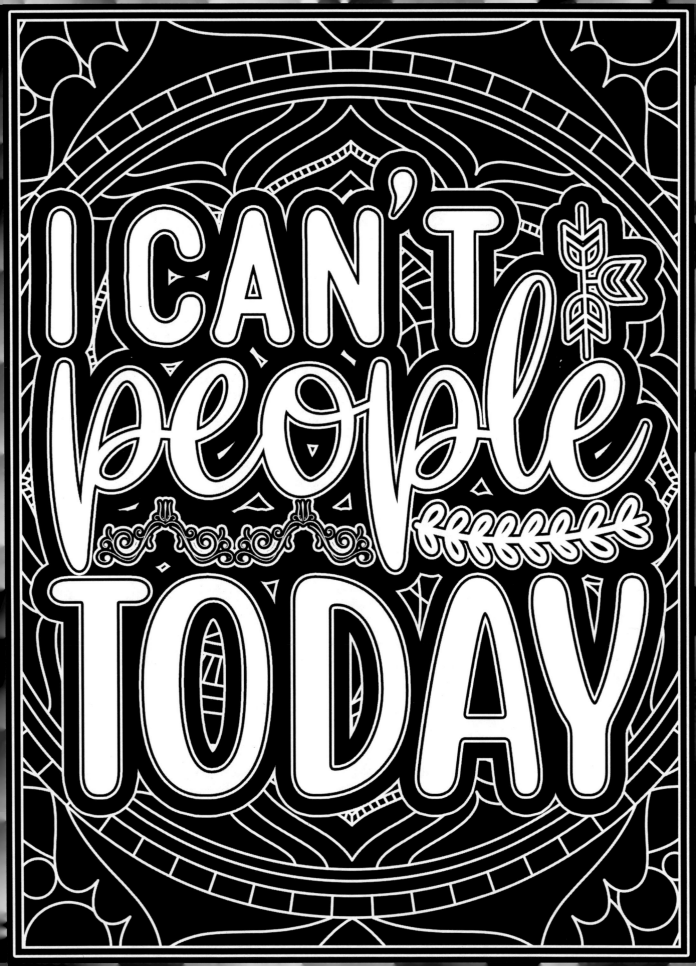

Tag us on your finished pages
for a free shoutout

Tag us on your finished pages
for a free shoutout

@BlackFeatherStationery

Tag us on your finished pages

for a free shoutout

@BlackFeatherStationery

Tag us on your finished pages

for a free shoutout

@BlackFeatherStationery

Tag us on your finished pages
for a free shoutout

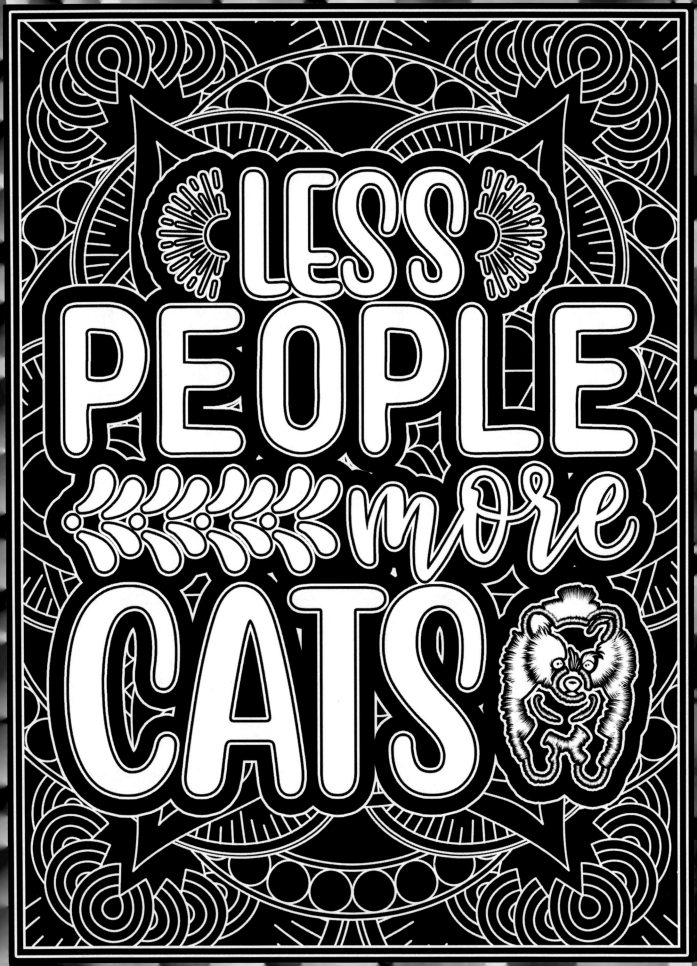

Tag us on your finished pages
for a free shoutout

@BlackFeatherStationery

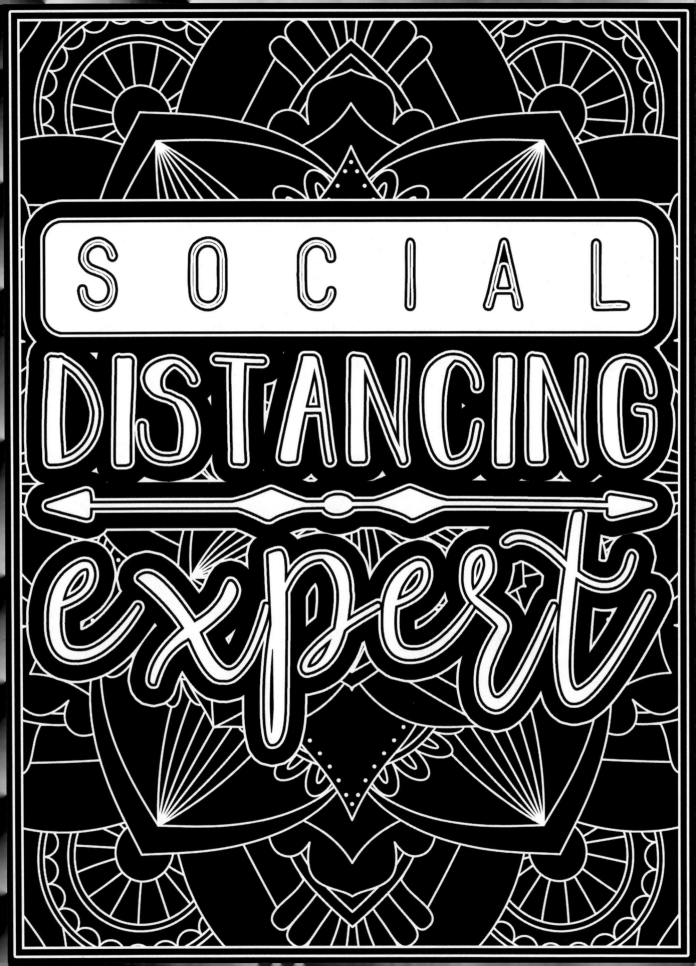

Tag us on your finished pages
for a free shoutout

 @BlackFeatherStationery

Tag us on your finished pages
for a free shoutout

@BlackFeatherStationery

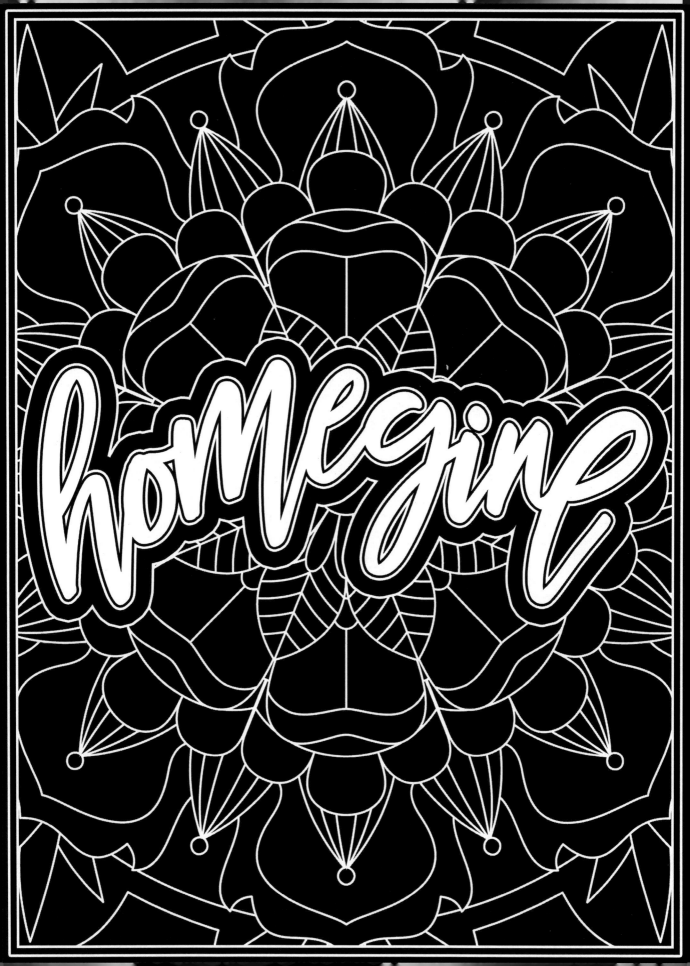

Tag us on your finished pages
for a free shoutout

@BlackFeatherStationery

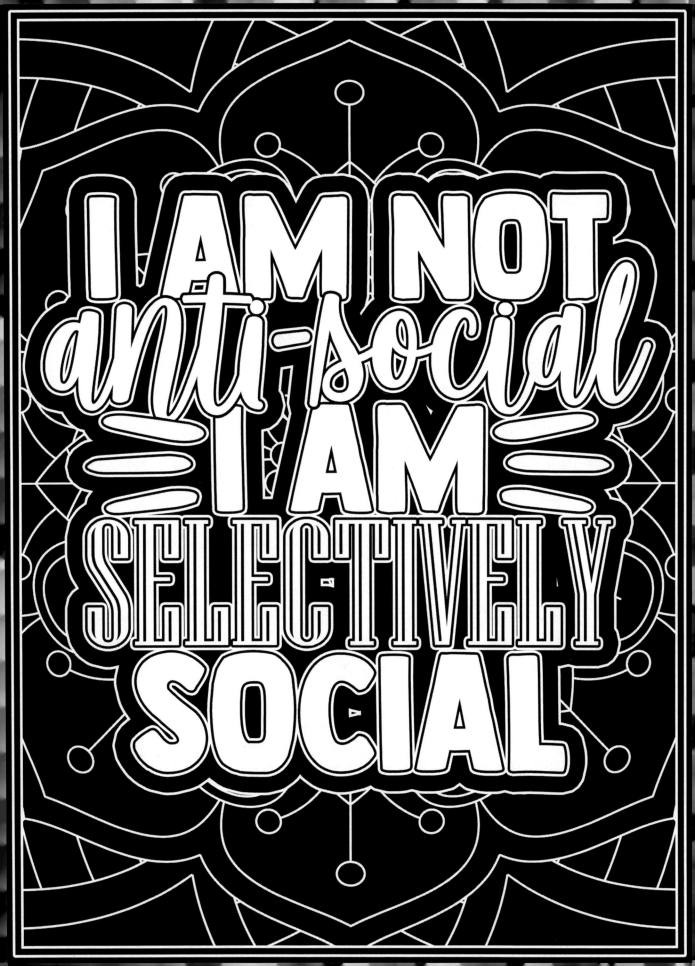

Tag us on your finished pages
for a free shoutout

 @BlackFeatherStationery

Tag us on your finished pages
for a free shoutout

@BlackFeatherStationery

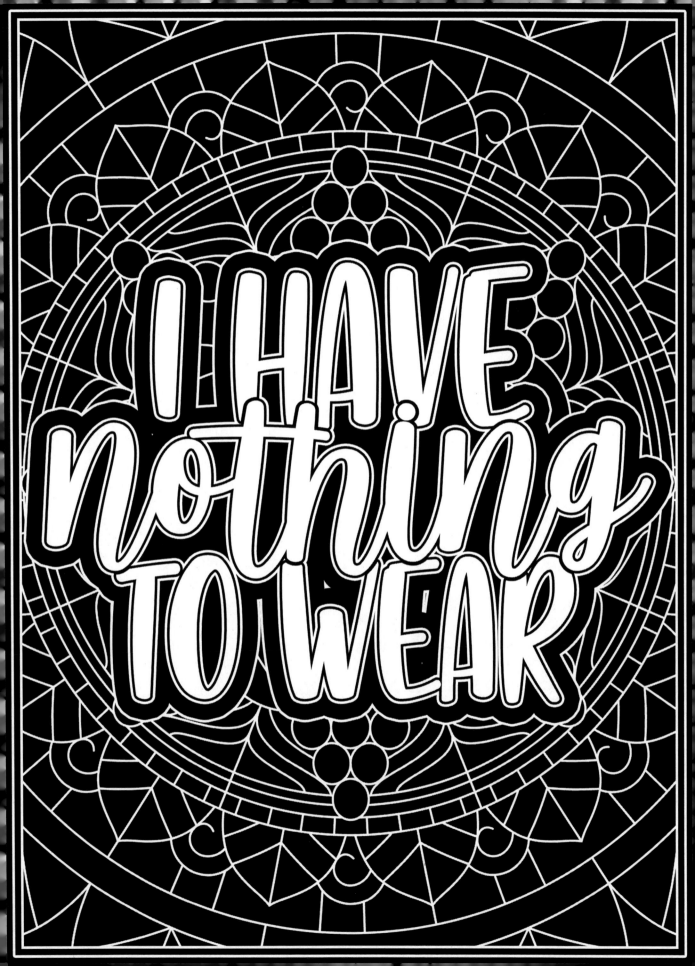

@ @BlackFeatherStationery

♥ 30 ♟ 5

Tag us on your finished pages
for a free shoutout

Tag us on your finished pages
for a free shoutout
@BlackFeatherStationery

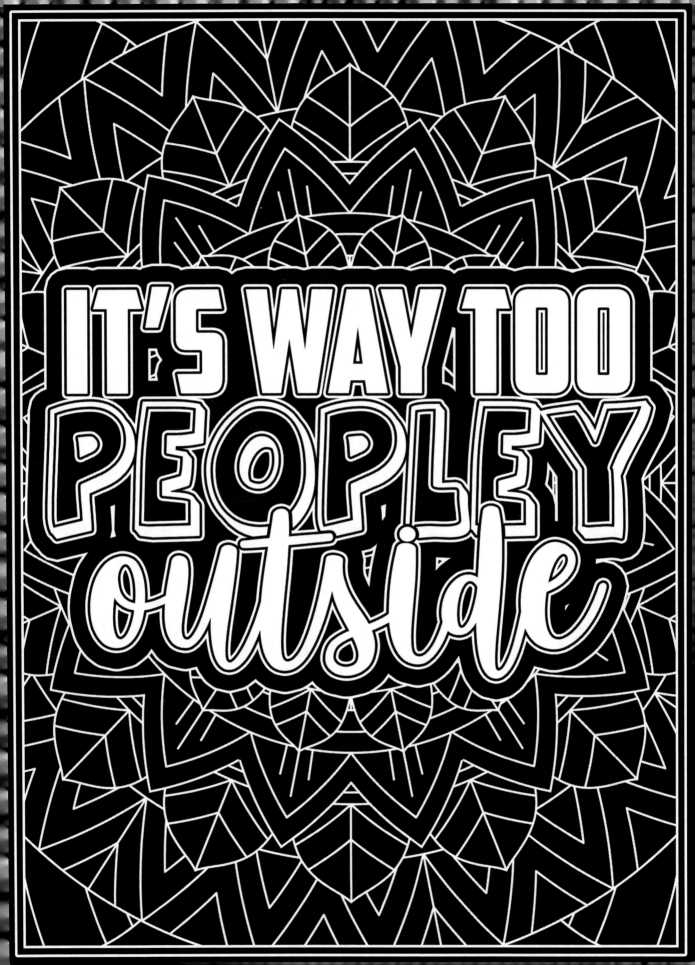

Tag us on your finished pages
for a free shoutout

@BlackFeatherStationery

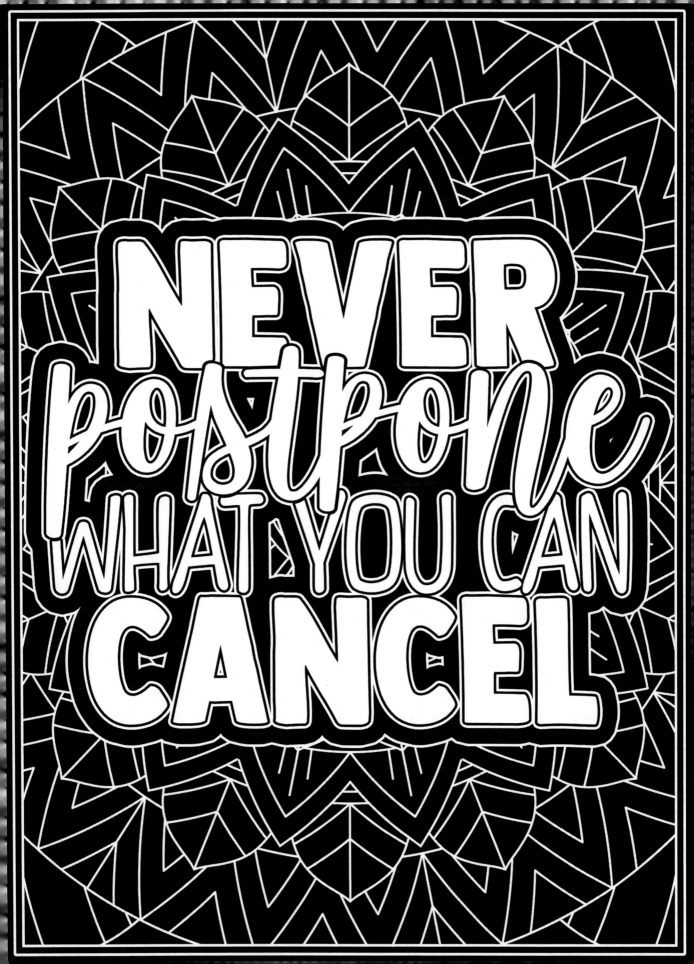

Tag us on your finished pages
for a free shoutout

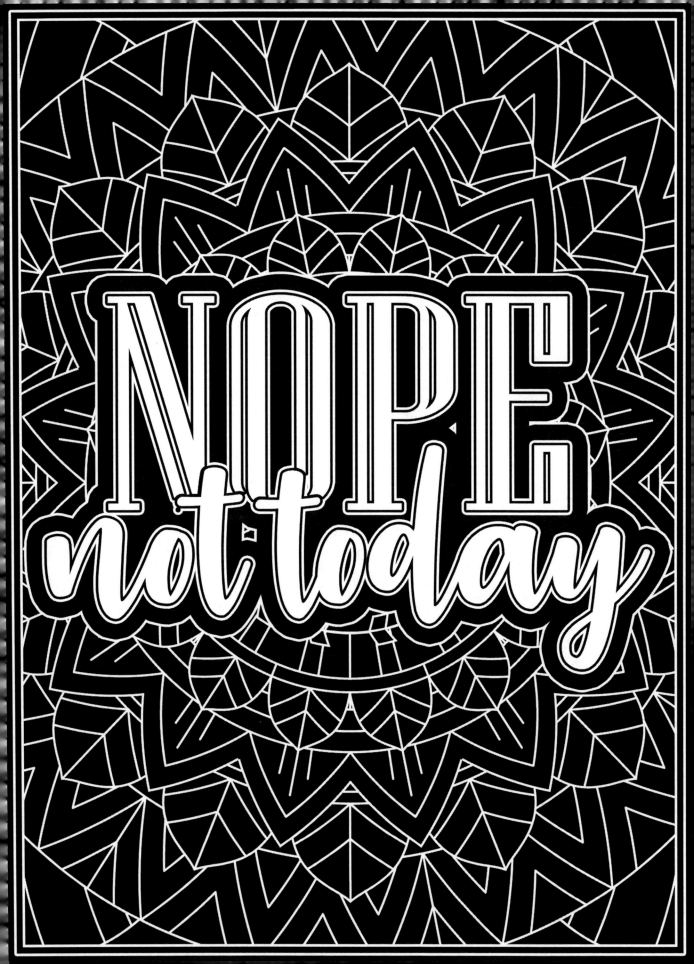

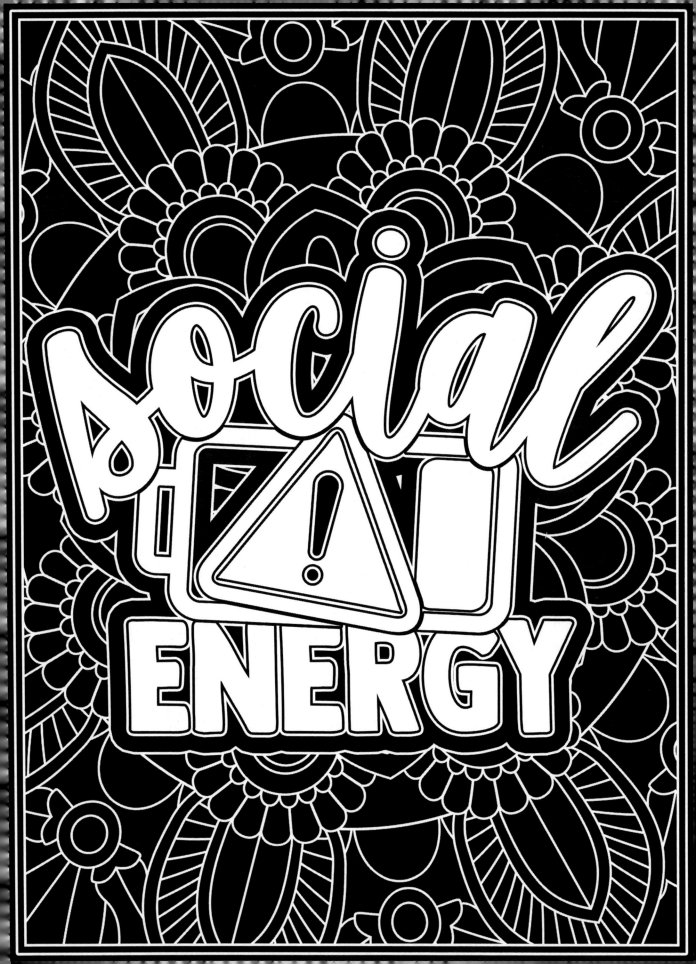

Tag us on your finished pages

for a free shoutout

@BlackFeatherStationery

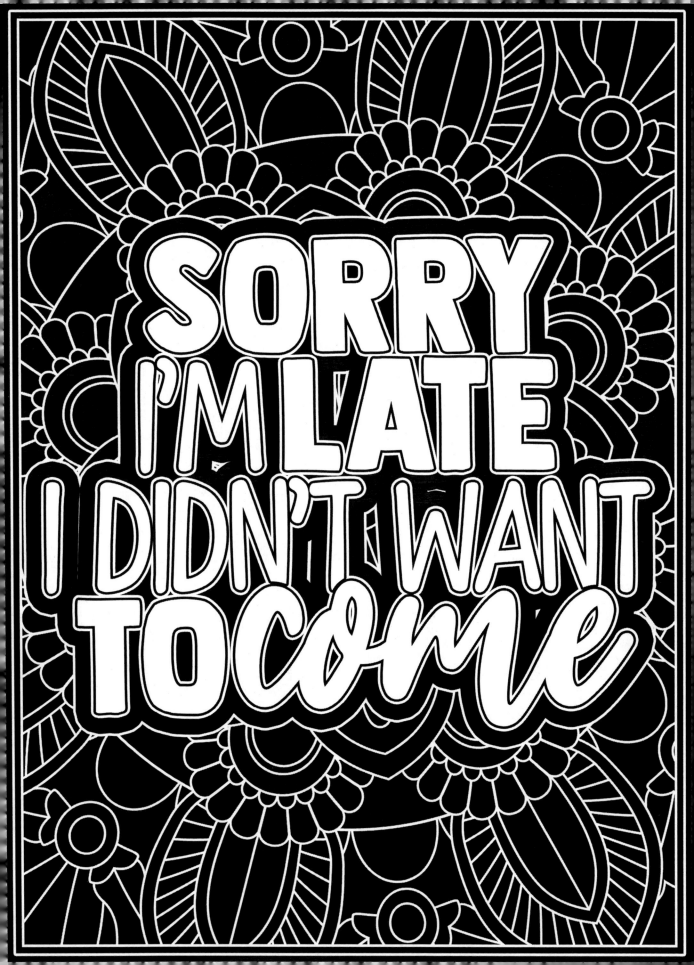

for a free shoutout

Tag us on your finished pages
for a free shoutout

 @BlackFeatherStationery

Tag us on your finished pages
for a free shoutout

Tag us on your finished pages
for a free shoutout

@BlackFeatherStationery

Tag us on your finished pages
for a free shoutout

@BlackFeatherStationery

Tag us on your finished pages
for a free shoutout

 @BlackFeatherStationery

Tag us on your finished pages
for a free shoutout

 @BlackFeatherStationery

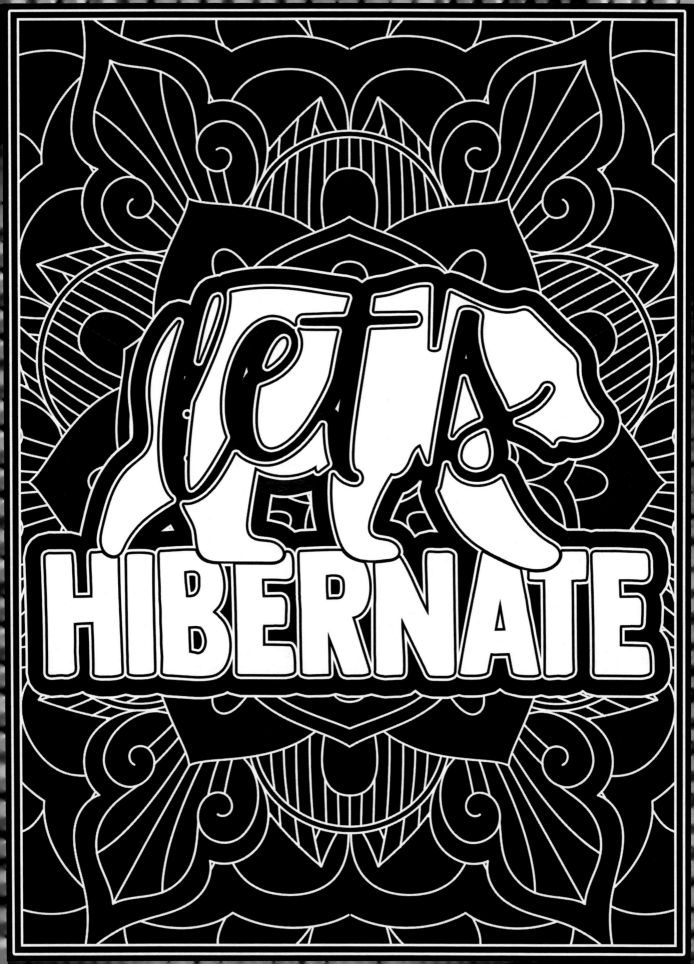

Tag us on your finished pages
for a free shoutout

📷 @BlackFeatherStationery

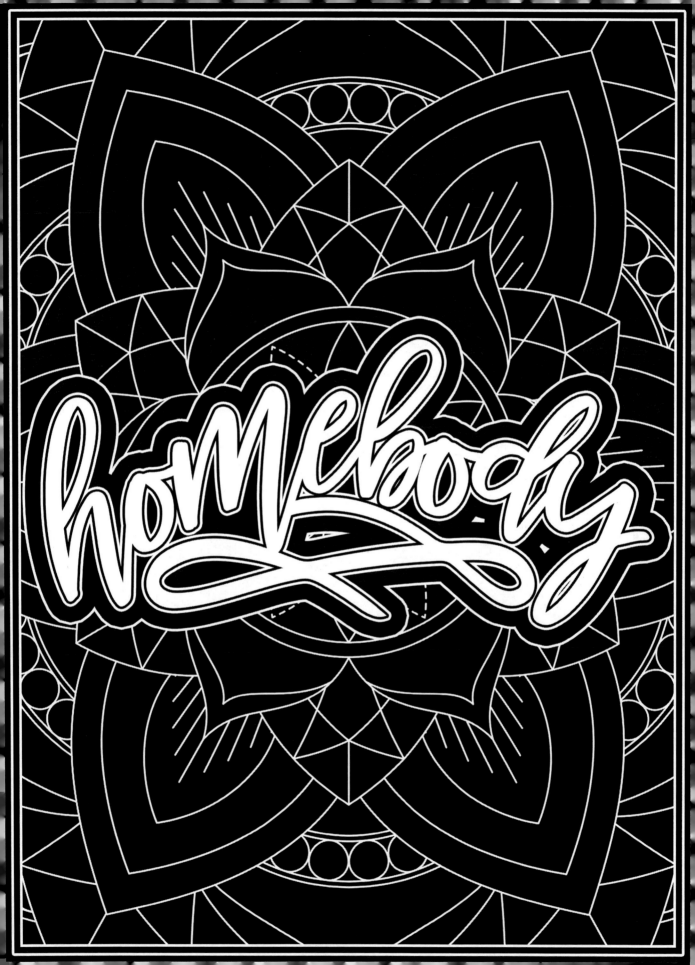

Tag us on your finished pages
for a free shoutout

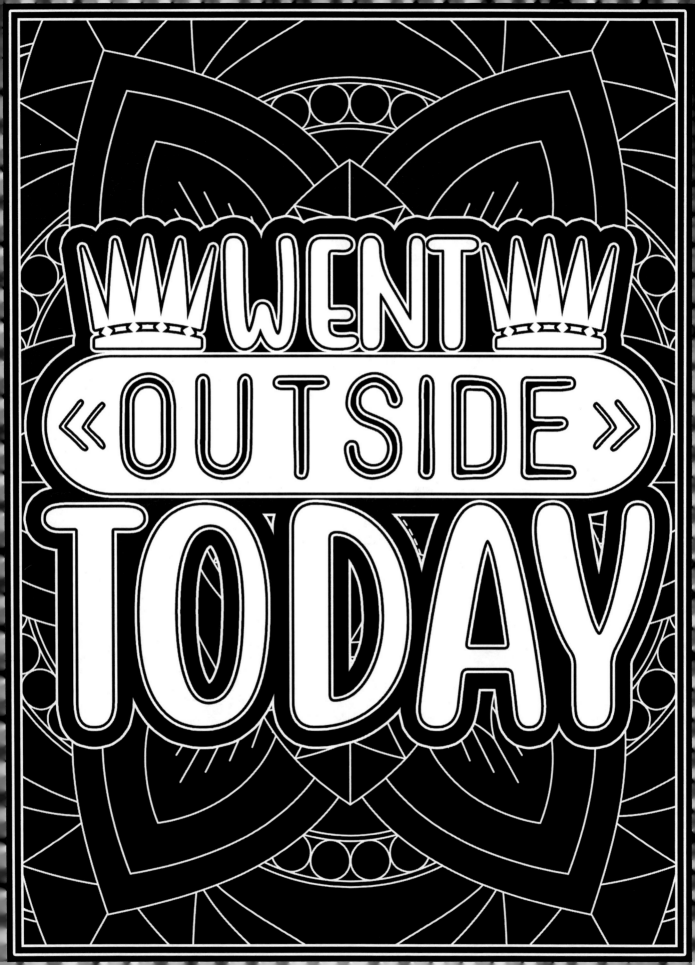

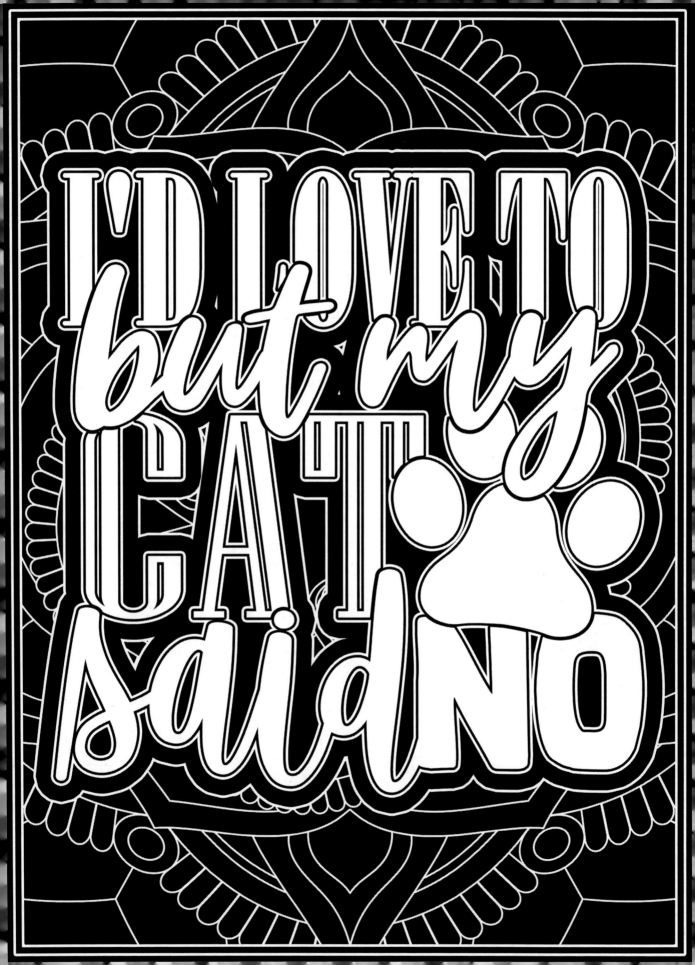

Tag us on your finished pages
for a free shoutout

@BlackFeatherStationery

Manufactured by Amazon.ca
Acheson, AB

14912681R00057